THE WORLD OF MIXED MARTIAL ARTS

INSIDE THE CAGE

THE GREATEST FIGHTS OF mixed martial arts

BY JIM WHITING

Consultant:
Robert Rousseau
Martial Arts Guide, *About.com*
Senior Writer, *MMAFighting.com*

Capstone press®

Mankato, Minnesota

Velocity is published by Capstone Press,
151 Good Counsel Drive, P.O. Box 669, Mankato, Minnesota 56002.
www.capstonepress.com

Books published by Capstone Press are manufactured with paper
containing at least 10 percent post-consumer waste.

Library of Congress Cataloging-in-Publication Data
Whiting, Jim, 1943–
 Inside the cage : the greatest fights of mixed martial arts / by Jim Whiting.
 p. cm. — (Velocity — the world of mixed martial arts)
 Includes bibliographical references and index.
 Summary: "Discusses some of the best mixed martial arts fights in the sport's history
and how MMA managed to survive its dark days" — Provided by publisher.
 ISBN 978-1-4296-3426-7 (library binding)
 1. Mixed martial arts — History — Juvenile literature. I. Title. II. Series.
GV1102.7.M59W54 2010
796.8 — dc22   2009007344

Editorial Credits
Abby Czeskleba, editor; Kyle Grenz, designer; Eric Gohl, media researcher

Photo Credits
AP Images/Eric Jamison, 18–19, 24; AP Images/Jon Super, 42; AP Images/Kyodo News,
16–17; AP Images/Laura Rauch, 22–23; AP Images/Marlene Karas, 38–39; AP Images/
MC, 9; AP Images/Rich Schultz, 43, 44–45; Capstone Press/Karon Dubke, 6–7; Corbis/
Sygma/Evan Hurd, 10–11, 13; Getty Images Inc./Jeff Hutchens, 14–15; Getty Images Inc./
Jon Kopaloff, 30–31; Getty Images Inc./Markus Boesch, 8; Getty Images Inc./WireImage/
Wendi Kaminski, 26–27; Landov LLC/CSM/John Pyle, 32–33; Landov LLC/Francis
Specker, 40–41; Newscom/CSM/John Pyle, 34–35; Newscom/Icon SMI/John Pyle, 20–21;
Newscom/Icon SMI/Zuma Press/Barry Sweet, 25; Newscom, 37; Newscom/UPI Photo/
Roger Williams, 28–29; Shutterstock/istera, 45 (scale); Shutterstock/keellla (chain link,
throughout); Shutterstock/Skocko, 12; Wikimedia/Lee Brimelow, cover, 4–5

TABLE OF CONTENTS

FIGHT NIGHT

Loud cheers of excited mixed martial arts (MMA) fans fill the air as two fighters enter the Octagon. The referee asks both fighters if they are ready. Another Ultimate Fighting Championship (UFC) fight is about to begin.

FACT: The Octagon's hand-painted canvas is changed after every event.

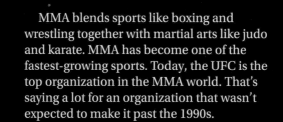

MMA blends sports like boxing and wrestling together with martial arts like judo and karate. MMA has become one of the fastest-growing sports. Today, the UFC is the top organization in the MMA world. That's saying a lot for an organization that wasn't expected to make it past the 1990s.

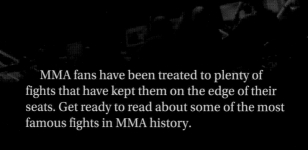

MMA fans have been treated to plenty of fights that have kept them on the edge of their seats. Get ready to read about some of the most famous fights in MMA history.

IN THE BEGINNING

Long before the UFC began, Helio Gracie created Brazilian Jiu-Jitsu (BJJ). BJJ would one day be a major fighting style in the UFC. While growing up, Gracie watched his older brothers teach jiu-jitsu. But he was too weak to practice the martial art himself. Gracie took jiu-jitsu skills that focused on upper-arm strength and adapted them because his legs were stronger than his arms. Brazilian Jiu-Jitsu focuses on grappling, ground fighting, and submission holds.

During grappling, a fighter controls his opponent with throws and holds.

Ground fighting involves the action that takes place on the mat. Fighters use different guard positions and submission holds during ground fighting.

Brazilian jiu-jitsu became very popular in Brazil. Helio's oldest son, Rorion, helped develop the UFC as a way to bring BJJ to the United States.

The first UFC event took place on November 12, 1993, in Denver, Colorado. UFC 1 was set up as an eight-man tournament. The final two fighters competed in the championship round for the $50,000 prize.

The UFC matched fighters from different fighting backgrounds. The purpose of UFC 1 was to determine the best fighting style and crown the Ultimate Fighter.

FACT: Traditional jiu-jitsu began several centuries ago in Japan. The martial art uses throws, holds, and strikes.

submission hold — a chokehold, joint hold, or compression lock

ROYCE GRACIE

The Gracies chose Royce Gracie to represent the family at UFC 1. Gracie stood about 6 feet (1.8 meters) tall and weighed 180 pounds (82 kilograms). The other seven fighters at UFC 1 outweighed Royce. The Gracies wanted to prove that a smaller man could defeat heavier opponents with Brazilian Jiu-Jitsu.

Helio Gracie proudly stood next to his son Royce after he won UFC 1. Royce became the first UFC champion and proved that Brazilian Jiu-Jitsu was superior to other fighting styles.

W.O.W. PROMOTIONS

12 NOV 19

Ultimate Fighter!

$ 5

00

x x

ousand

One of Royce's opponents was boxer Art Jimmerson. Jimmerson tapped out less than three minutes into the match. This was Gracie's longest match of the night. He used submission holds to defeat his other two opponents.

THE BOXER
vs.
THE WRESTLER

In 1976, famous boxer Muhammad Ali fought in one of the first MMA-style matches. He took on Japanese wrestler Antonio Inoki in Tokyo, Japan.

Ali thought the fight would be a joke because both men had planned their moves before the match. Then he found out that Inoki wanted to make the match into a real fight. Ali made sure the rules didn't allow Inoki to use wrestling moves. Ali didn't want Inoki to have an advantage.

The match was very boring. Inoki spent most of the 15 rounds on one knee or his back. He kicked at Ali's legs. Ali couldn't get close to him. His first punch came during the seventh round. Ali had just six punches during the entire fight. Neither Ali nor Inoki won, and the match was ruled a draw.

BRAZILIAN JIU-JITSU is KING

Royce Gracie was the top UFC fighter after winning the first two UFC events. He dropped out of UFC 3 due to exhaustion and dehydration. But two championships weren't enough, and he decided to go back for a third title at UFC 4. He fought one of the toughest opponents of his career during the final match of UFC 4. Dan Severn was an experienced wrestler. He also had close to a 100-pound (45-kilogram) advantage over Gracie. Severn entered the Octagon for the first time at UFC 4. The two men battled for the championship that night.

Severn took Gracie to the canvas early in the match. Gracie used the closed guard to defend himself. He wrapped his legs around Severn's back. Much of the fight was spent on the ground.

Severn controlled most of the match. Things didn't look good for Gracie. But the tables soon turned in Gracie's favor when he put Severn into a triangle choke. The match ended when Severn tapped out. The fight lasted close to 16 minutes. At the time, it was Gracie's longest UFC fight. Royce's win against Severn had once again proven that the Gracies' style of fighting could beat anyone.

Royce Gracie and Ken Shamrock first squared off at UFC 1 on November 12, 1993.

FACT: Royce Gracie wore his Brazilian Jiu-Jitsu *gi* (GEE) during his matches. Today's UFC fighters all wear shorts and gloves.

Royce Gracie fought Ken Shamrock at UFC 1. Shamrock took down Gracie early in the match. But Gracie quickly escaped and put a chokehold on his opponent. Shamrock was angry about being defeated so quickly. He wanted a second fight with Gracie. Shamrock finally got his chance at UFC 5 on April 7, 1995.

THE REMATCH

UFC promoters didn't want either man to lose in an early round of the tournament. They added a Gracie-Shamrock "super fight" to the fight card. More than 250,000 people purchased UFC 5 on pay-per-view (PPV), an amazing number for a new sport.

By the time of UFC 5, Shamrock and a few other fighters had learned how to defend themselves against Gracie's moves. Royce Gracie's advantage was starting to disappear.

Fights lasted longer than before because many UFC fighters had evenly matched skills. These fights outlasted the PPV time limit. As a result, UFC officials set a 30-minute time limit.

But on this particular night, 30 minutes was not enough time to declare a winner. Fans started booing after 20 minutes passed without much action.

When the fight reached the time limit, officials added five minutes. There was still no winner after 35 minutes. Boos filled the arena as the referee stopped the match. The fight was called a draw.

PROBLEMS BEGIN

As a UFC showcase event, the Gracie-Shamrock "super fight" was a failure. The lack of action and no clear winner turned off a lot of fans to the brutal sport.

To prevent future draws, the UFC added judges. Three judges would determine the outcome of matches that reached the time limit without a winner. These new rules angered the Gracies. In Brazil, they competed in *vale tudo* matches. There were no rules or time limits in this fighting style. The family left the UFC and took Royce Gracie, the UFC's first big name, with them.

It was bad enough that the UFC had lost its most famous fighter. But it soon had to deal with a much more serious problem.

FACT: *Vale tudo* means "anything goes" in Portuguese.

DARK DAYS

UFC owners boasted that there were no rules during the organization's early days. Two fighters entered the Octagon, but only one fighter could leave. The other fighter would be left bruised and battered in the middle of the cage.

But the same no-holds-barred matches that put the UFC on the map began causing problems. Many people believed that any "real" sport needed rules.

One of those people was Senator John McCain. He thought MMA was too violent. In the mid-1990s, he wrote letters to the 50 state governors asking them to ban the sport. McCain also encouraged big PPV providers to stop showing MMA fights on TV.

Because of McCain's actions, fewer places were available for UFC fights. Major PPV providers stopped carrying UFC events and fewer people tuned in.

PRIDE FIGHTING CHAMPIONSHIPS

MMA was clearly struggling in the United States, but the sport's popularity was growing in Japan. PRIDE Fighting Championships held its first event on October 11, 1997. PRIDE 1 attracted more than 47,000 fans.

Two fighters duke it out during a PRIDE Fighting Championships match.

The main event featured popular Japanese wrestler Nobuhiko Takada. Takada's opponent was Rickson Gracie, one of Royce's older brothers. Rickson practiced his family's art, BJJ, while Takada was a professional wrestler. Both men argued that their fighting style was superior.

But the talking stopped when the action started. Gracie won the match when he forced Takada into an armbar. Gracie won the fight in less than five minutes.

16

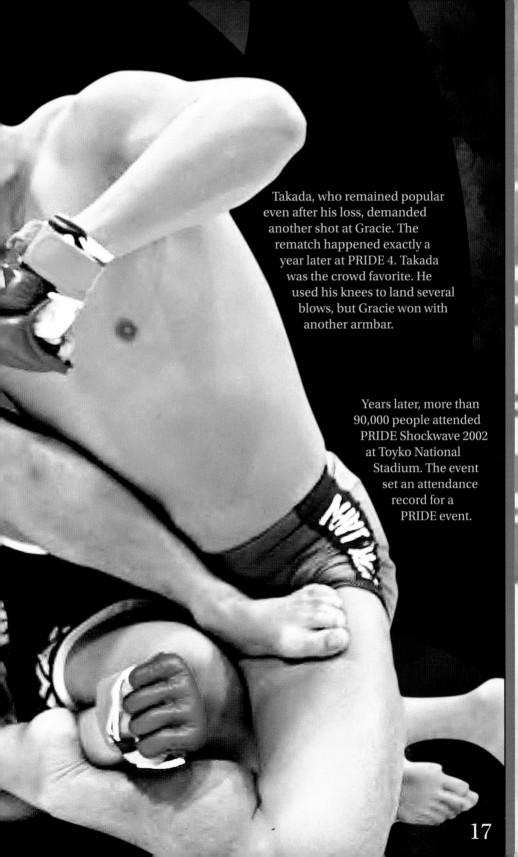

Takada, who remained popular even after his loss, demanded another shot at Gracie. The rematch happened exactly a year later at PRIDE 4. Takada was the crowd favorite. He used his knees to land several blows, but Gracie won with another armbar.

Years later, more than 90,000 people attended PRIDE Shockwave 2002 at Toyko National Stadium. The event set an attendance record for a PRIDE event.

The sport's hard times continued back in the United States, but there were signs of hope. In 2001, the Unified Rules of Mixed Martial Arts (URMMA) were formally adopted. MMA officials believed these rules would lead people to accept MMA as a real sport. Officials also hoped the rules would bring fans back to the sport.

Another sign of hope came early the following year. Brothers Lorenzo Fertitta and Frank Fertitta III, along with current UFC president Dana White, took over the UFC in 2001.

The Fertitta brothers became MMA fans after seeing their first MMA fight. They knew they were taking a big risk because the UFC had been steadily losing money. But the brothers still jumped at the chance to buy the UFC.

As new owners, the Fertittas increased the amount of advertising for events. They also held fights in bigger arenas. They talked large PPV companies into carrying the fights. As time passed, the UFC started to make more money. Today, the UFC is the largest MMA organization, which goes to show the Fertittas' risk paid off.

The three men formed the company Zuffa. UFC 30 was Zuffa's first event. The event was held at the Trump Taj Mahal, a famous resort in Atlantic City, New Jersey.

UFC owners Frank Fertitta III (left), Dana White (center), and Lorenzo Fertitta (right) helped the UFC survive its dark days.

FACT: *Zuffa* means "fight" in Italian.

19

The main event at UFC 30 featured middleweight champion Tito Ortiz and challenger Evan Tanner. Ortiz bodyslammed Tanner to the mat less than one minute into the first round.

Ortiz started punching even though Tanner was hardly conscious after the slam. The referee hurled himself at Ortiz to protect Tanner.

Ortiz

The referee's actions showed that fighter safety was important in the "new" UFC. It seemed that MMA was going to make it.

UFC 30:

Ortiz vs. Tanner
February 23, 2001

Location:
Atlantic City, New Jersey

Weight Class:
Middleweight
185.1–199 lb (84–90.2 kg)

Match ended:
30 secs. into Round 1
Win by knockout

FACT: Beginning with UFC 31, the middleweight class was renamed the light-heavyweight division.

MMA MAKES a COMEBACK

With the UFC's main problems in the rearview mirror, Zuffa could focus on regaining the UFC's former popularity. As a way to attract more fans, the UFC began playing up the rivalries among fighters.

Shamrock

ORTIZ vs. SHAMROCK

One of the most famous rivalries dated back several years between Shamrock and Ortiz. Shamrock ran a training center called the Lion's Den. Ortiz had defeated one of Shamrock's fighters in 1999. When Ortiz mocked the fighter, Shamrock took the insults personally. Ortiz and Shamrock agreed to settle their differences at UFC 40.

technical knockout — the act of stopping a fight when a fighter is at risk of serious injury if the fight continues

Fans looked forward to the light-heavyweight championship match. Ortiz had defended his title four times since winning it in early 2000.

This fifth defense would be equally successful. While Shamrock landed some good blows, Ortiz controlled the match. Shamrock's trainers stopped the fight because he was too injured to continue. Ortiz earned the technical knockout (TKO).

Ortiz

UFC 40:

Ortiz vs. Shamrock
November 22, 2002

Location:
Las Vegas, Nevada

Weight Class:
Light Heavyweight
185.1–205 lb (84–92.9 kg)

Match ended:
5 mins. into Round 3
Win by TKO

FACT: The fight between Ortiz and Shamrock at UFC 40 was advertised as "Vendetta." A vendetta is a long-lasting fight.

LIDDELL vs. COUTURE

Randy Couture won the heavyweight title in 1997. It was taken away in 1998 because of contract problems with the UFC. He fought in Japan and later returned to the United States. Couture regained his title in 2000. When he lost his championship two years later, he moved to the light-heavyweight class. He made the switch because he was one of the lighter fighters in the heavyweight class.

Couture's timing was good. When he switched weight classes, UFC officials were having a contract dispute with light-heavyweight champion Ortiz. Officials wanted Ortiz to take on the top light-heavyweight fighter, Chuck "The Iceman" Liddell.

Couture

When Ortiz refused to fight Liddell, UFC officials created a temporary light-heavyweight championship. Liddell would fight Couture for the title at UFC 43. People called Couture the underdog. They thought losing weight to switch weight classes would make him weaker. Liddell's 12-1 record also made him a fan favorite.

To people's surprise, Couture controlled the fight from the beginning. During the third round, he took Liddell to the canvas and began punching him. The referee quickly stopped the fight. Couture became the first man in UFC history to win titles in two weight classes. Months later, Couture defeated Ortiz to remove any doubt about his right to the light-heavyweight title.

Liddell

UFC 43:

Liddell vs. Couture
June 6, 2003

Location:
Las Vegas, Nevada

Weight Class:
Light Heavyweight
185.1–205 lb (84–92.9 kg)

Match ended:
2 mins., 40 secs.
into Round 3
Win by TKO

HUGHES vs. PENN

B.J. Penn became popular as a lightweight fighter. He moved up a weight division to challenge Matt Hughes for the welterweight title at UFC 46. Hughes won his title at UFC 34 and successfully defended it five times before UFC 46. Both fighters threw punches early on in the first round before the action moved to the canvas. While Hughes was known for his takedowns, he didn't have the strongest ground game.

Hughes

Penn knew his opponent's weakness. He kept Hughes from standing up and gaining the advantage. To defend himself, Hughes took the open guard position. Penn passed guard with a hard blow to his opponent's face. Penn then mounted Hughes. Hughes made his biggest mistake when he tried to escape Penn's mount by rolling. Seconds later, Penn ended the fight with a chokehold.

Penn, the underdog at UFC 46, had become the welterweight champion. But the UFC stripped him of his title when he signed with a different MMA organization later that year.

Penn came back to the UFC in 2006 as a welterweight. He lost a rematch to Hughes at UFC 63 shortly after his return.

UFC 46:

Hughes vs. Penn
January 31, 2004

Location:
Las Vegas, Nevada

Weight Class:
Welterweight
155.1–170 lb (70.4–77.1 kg)

Match ended:
4 mins., 39 secs.
into Round 1
Win by submission

Penn

FACT: Many fans believe the Hughes-Penn rematch at UFC 63 was one of the greatest fights in UFC history.

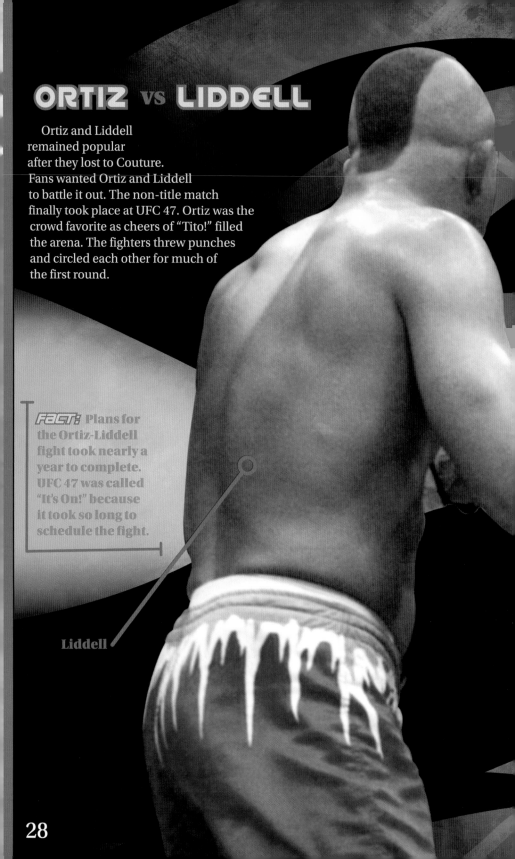

ORTIZ vs LIDDELL

Ortiz and Liddell remained popular after they lost to Couture. Fans wanted Ortiz and Liddell to battle it out. The non-title match finally took place at UFC 47. Ortiz was the crowd favorite as cheers of "Tito!" filled the arena. The fighters threw punches and circled each other for much of the first round.

FACT: Plans for the Ortiz-Liddell fight took nearly a year to complete. UFC 47 was called "It's On!" because it took so long to schedule the fight.

Liddell

Liddell accidentally poked Ortiz in the eye early in the second round. Liddell's punches went unanswered as Ortiz protected his face with his arms. The flurry of punches was too much for Ortiz. The referee stepped in to stop the action, and Liddell earned a TKO.

Ortiz

UFC 47:

Ortiz vs. Liddell
April 2, 2004

Location:
Las Vegas, Nevada

Weight Class:
Light Heavyweight
185.1–205 lb (84–92.9 kg)

Match ended:
38 secs. into Round 2
Win by TKO

At this point, fans still had to pay for UFC events on pay-per-view. But with the sport's popularity growing, that was about to change. Soon, a whole new audience would be introduced to MMA.

THE *GROWTH* CONTINUES

In 2000, reality TV shows like *Survivor* sparked interest among millions of viewers. The Fertittas wanted to tap into this popularity. They thought an MMA reality show would bring new fans to the sport.

A TOUGH SELL

Networks didn't jump at the idea of an MMA reality TV show. The Fertittas approached several networks. No one was interested in airing the show. Then the brothers agreed to pay the millions of dollars it would cost to make the show. The cable network Spike TV decided to broadcast *The Ultimate Fighter* (*TUF*) in January 2005. Anyone with cable could watch the show without paying extra money.

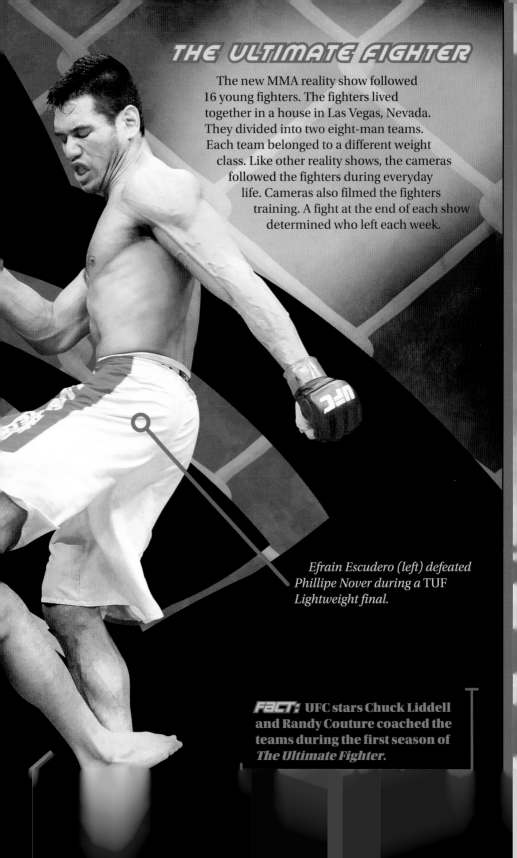

THE ULTIMATE FIGHTER

The new MMA reality show followed 16 young fighters. The fighters lived together in a house in Las Vegas, Nevada. They divided into two eight-man teams. Each team belonged to a different weight class. Like other reality shows, the cameras followed the fighters during everyday life. Cameras also filmed the fighters training. A fight at the end of each show determined who left each week.

Efrain Escudero (left) defeated Phillipe Nover during a TUF Lightweight final.

FACT: UFC stars Chuck Liddell and Randy Couture coached the teams during the first season of *The Ultimate Fighter*.

TUF's last show aired on April 9, 2005. There were finals in both weight classes, plus a "super fight" between Shamrock and rising star Rich Franklin.

The first final featured *The Ultimate Fighter* middleweights Diego Sanchez and Kenny Florian. Sanchez scored a TKO halfway through the first round.

Griffin

But the best fight of the night was between light heavyweights Forrest Griffin and Stephan Bonnar. Both men landed punch after punch during the action-packed match. It was clear their skills were perfectly matched.

The TV announcers called the match one of the best fights they had ever seen. The action continued into the final round.

Both men were still standing at the end of the third round. In a 29-28 unanimous decision, the judges declared Griffin the winner. Griffin had won all three rounds. But Dana White told both fighters there was no loser in the match. He offered Griffin and Bonnar UFC contracts. When *The Ultimate Fighter* began, the contract had only been planned for the winner.

Nearly 3 million viewers watched the last show of the season. White later said that the Griffin-Bonnar fight was the most important in UFC history.

FACT: Forrest Griffin won the UFC light-heavyweight championship in 2008.

COUTURE vs LIDDELL:
The Rematches

Just a week after *The Ultimate Fighter* ended, the UFC made history again. Nearly 300,000 fans watched UFC 52 on PPV, the highest total at the time. Zuffa had used *The Ultimate Fighter* to lead up to the rematch between Couture and Liddell. Their rematch would decide the light-heavyweight championship, a title held by Couture leading up to UFC 52.

The two men traded blows back and forth before entering a **clinch** against the fence. Couture was holding his right eye after the clinch ended. The referee halted the action while the fight doctor took care of Couture. Shortly after the match started up again, Liddell knocked out Couture with a punch to the jaw. The knockout ended the match in the first round. Liddell became the new light-heavyweight champion.

Liddell

UFC 52:

Couture vs. Liddell
April 16, 2005

Location:
Las Vegas, Nevada

Weight Class:
Light Heavyweight
185.1–205 lb (84–92.9 kg)

Match ended:
2 mins., 6 secs.
into Round 1
Win by knockout

TURNING THE TABLES

The Couture-Liddell rematch wasn't the only exciting fight of the night. UFC 52 also featured a welterweight championship fight between challenger Frank Trigg and champion Matt Hughes.

Trigg accidentally kneed Hughes in the groin during the first round, but the referee didn't see the foul. When Hughes turned to complain to the referee, Trigg pounded him. After forcing Hughes to the canvas, Trigg put him into a chokehold.

Trigg may have had an unfair advantage, but the referee didn't stop the match. Trigg kept fighting because that's what he had been trained to do. Somehow Hughes managed to escape the chokehold. He got to his feet, picked up Trigg, and slammed him to the mat. Trigg was forced to submit after Hughes put him in a chokehold. Many fans consider Hughes' victory to be one of the greatest comebacks in MMA history.

FACT: Fighters may enter a clinch for many reasons. A clinch protects against strikes and allows both men to take a break from the action. Fighters who have mastered the clinch may throw short strikes or use knee strikes to weaken an opponent.

clinch — a position in which two fighters stand face to face, usually with their arms and upper bodies locked together

LIDDELL vs COUTURE

Couture and Liddell weren't through with each other after UFC 52. They met again at UFC 57 on February 4, 2006. Liddell was still the light-heavyweight champion going into this third and final fight between the bitter rivals.

The two men circled each other for much of the first round. The first few minutes were full of missed punches. The action picked up toward the end of the round when Couture took Liddell to the mat. Less than five seconds later, Liddell was on his feet again. Liddell opened a cut above Couture's eye in the first round. Couture's trainers treated the bloody cut during the break.

As the second round began, it seemed Couture was at a disadvantage. The commentators wondered if Couture had a broken nose. The injury would force him to breathe out of his mouth. Liddell's strikes to the face would be more dangerous with Couture's open jaw.

The two men traded punches when suddenly Couture lost his footing. Liddell caught him in the neck with a right-hand punch. But Liddell didn't stop there. When Couture fell to the canvas, Liddell rained down punches until the referee stopped the match. Liddell had knocked out Couture less than two minutes into the second round. That night, Couture announced his retirement from the UFC.

Couture

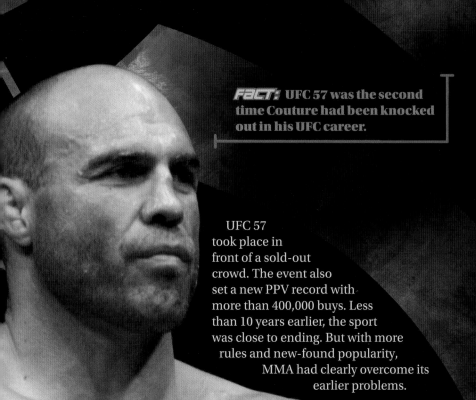

FACT: UFC 57 was the second time Couture had been knocked out in his UFC career.

UFC 57 took place in front of a sold-out crowd. The event also set a new PPV record with more than 400,000 buys. Less than 10 years earlier, the sport was close to ending. But with more rules and new-found popularity, MMA had clearly overcome its earlier problems.

UFC 57:

Liddell vs. Couture
February 4, 2006

Location:
Las Vegas, Nevada

Weight Class:
Light Heavyweight
185.1–205 lb (84–92.9 kg)

Match ended:
1 min., 28 secs.
into Round 2
Win by knockout

CHAPTER 5

INTO THE SPOTLIGHT

Anyone doubting MMA's popularity only had to look at the sales for UFC 66 on December 30, 2006.

Liddell

The **live gate** for the event was more than $5 million, almost $2 million more than the live gate for UFC 57. There were more than 1 million PPV buys for UFC 66.

live gate — the total amount of money paid by a live audience to watch an event

LIDDELL vs. ORTIZ

UFC 66 featured a rematch between Liddell and Ortiz. Liddell knocked Ortiz down in the first round and opened up a cut above Ortiz's eye. Ortiz kept fighting and scored a takedown in the second round.

When Liddell scrambled back to his feet, he knocked down Ortiz again. Liddell's blow reopened the cut above Ortiz's eye. The referee stopped the fight with a minute left in the third round. Liddell earned the TKO.

Ortiz

UFC 66:

Liddell vs. Ortiz
December 30, 2006

Location:
Las Vegas, Nevada

Weight Class:
Light Heavyweight
185.1–205 lb (84–92.9 kg)

Match ended:
3 mins., 59 secs.
into Round 3
Win by TKO

SYLVIA VS. COUTURE

Couture's retirement was short-lived. He moved to the heavyweight class after coming back to the UFC. Couture faced Tim Sylvia for the heavyweight title at UFC 68.

The odds of winning the fight were in Sylvia's favor. Sylvia stood 6 inches (15 centimeters) taller than his opponent. Sylvia outweighed Couture by more than 40 pounds (18 kilograms). Sylvia was also 12 years younger than Couture.

UFC 68:

Sylvia vs. Couture
March 3, 2007

Location:
Columbus, Ohio

Weight Class:
**Heavyweight
205.1–265 lb (93–120.2 kg)**

Match ended:
**5 mins. into Round 5
Win by
unanimous decision**

Sylvia

Couture wasted no time when the fight began. He knocked Sylvia to the canvas less than 10 seconds into the first round. When Sylvia got up, Couture took him down again. The fighters spent most of the first round on the ground. The action picked up in the rounds that followed.

When the fifth round ended, the crowd went wild as Couture raised his hands in victory. "This place is deafening!" shouted one commentator. Couture knew he had won the match even before it was official. When the winner was announced, it was no surprise. Couture won the match by unanimous decision.

Couture

FACT: Couture became the oldest fighter to win a UFC championship.

PENN vs. STEVENSON

B.J. Penn faced Joe Stevenson for the lightweight title at UFC 80. An elbow to the face opened a cut above Stevenson's left eye toward the end of the first round. Stevenson's forehead was covered in blood. Stevenson's trainers treated the cut during the break, but the bleeding started up again in the second round.

Penn and Stevenson traded punches early in the second round. Halfway through the round, Penn took a bloody Stevenson to the canvas. The rest of the fight stayed on the ground as Penn used a chokehold that caused Stevenson to tap out.

Stevenson

UFC 80:

**Penn vs. Stevenson
January 19, 2008**

**Location:
Newcastle, England**

**Weight Class:
Lightweight
145.1–155 lb (65.8–70.3 kg)**

Penn

**Match ended:
4 mins., 2 secs.
into Round 2
Win by submission**

FACT: Penn was the second fighter to win championships in two weight classes.

SLICE vs. THOMPSON

On May 31, 2008, CBS broadcast an MMA show produced by Elite Xtreme Combat (Elite XC). Normally shows like this one were only available on PPV. The main event matched Kimbo Slice and James Thompson. Fans knew Slice from watching street fights on the Internet.

It was just Slice's third MMA fight. Thompson had more than 20 MMA fights to his credit.

Slice

Thompson

During the second round, Thompson sat on top of Slice while punching him several times. Some fans felt the fight should have stopped at this point. Other fights had ended in situations like this, but the referee let the match continue this time.

ELITE XC:

**Slice vs. Thompson
May 31, 2008**

**Location:
Newark, New Jersey**

**Weight Class:
Heavyweight
205.1–265 lb (93–120.2 kg)**

**Match ended:
36 secs. into Round 3
Win by TKO**

Thompson lost control of the match in the third round. Blood gushed out of his ear after one of Slice's punches. Slice scored a TKO to end the match.

CARANO vs. YOUNG

People thought the best match of the Elite XC fight card featured Gina Carano and Kaitlin Young. It was the first serious TV coverage for female MMA fighters. Most fans felt that Young won the first round. But the heavily favored Carano took control in the second round. She knocked down Young with a kick and nearly forced her to submit. By that time, Young's left eye was swollen shut. Young lasted until the end of the second round, but her trainers threw in the towel before the final round began. Carano earned the TKO.

Young

At the weigh-in, Carano was over the 140-pound (63.5-kilogram) weight limit. As a result, she had to give part of her winnings to Young. But that didn't matter to the live crowd that chanted "Gina! Gina! Gina!" during the fight.

FACT: Gina Carano practices Muay Thai, the national sport of Thailand. Muay Thai is also called Thai boxing.

Carano

ELITE XC

Carano vs. Young
May 31, 2008

Location:
Newark, New Jersey

Weight Class:
140 lb (63.5 kg)

Match ended:
3 mins. into Round 2
Win by TKO

The hard-hitting action of MMA keeps fans coming back for more. The future is sure to be filled with fights worthy of the record books.

GLOSSARY

brutal (BROO-tuhl) — cruel and violent

clinch (KLINCH) — a position in which two fighters stand face to face, usually with their arms and upper bodies locked together

commentator (KOM-uhn-tey-ter) — a person who calls the action at a live sporting event

fight card (FITE KARD) — a list of matches during an MMA event

live gate (LIVE GATE) — the total amount of money paid by a live audience to watch an event

pay-per-view (PAY PUR VYOO) — a service for cable TV viewers in which customers order and view a single movie or televised event for a fee

reality TV show (ree-AL-uh-tee tee-VEE SHOH) — a TV show without any scripts or professional actors

rivalry (RYE-val-ree) — a fierce feeling of competition between two people

submission hold (suhb-MISH-uhn HOHLD) — a chokehold, joint hold, or compression lock that causes a fighter's opponent to end the match by tapping out or saying, "I submit."

takedown (TAYK-doun) — an action in which a fighter forces an opponent to the ground

technical knockout (TEK-nuh-kuhl NOK-out) — the act of stopping a fight when a fighter is at risk of serious injury if the fight continues

unanimous decision (yoo-NAN-uh-muhss di-SIZH-uhn) — a situation in which all three judges agree on a winner

read more

Franklin, Rich, and Jon F. Merz. *The Complete Idiot's Guide to Ultimate Fighting.* Indianapolis: Alpha, 2007.

Ollhoff, Jim. *Martial Arts Around the Globe.* The World of Martial Arts. Edina, Minn.: ABDO, 2008.

Ollhoff, Jim. *Martial Arts Movies.* The World of Martial Arts. Edina, Minn.: ABDO, 2008.

Shamrock, Frank. *Mixed Martial Arts for Dummies.* Indianapolis: Wiley, 2009.

INTERNET SITES

FactHound offers a safe, fun way to find Internet sites related to this book. All of the sites on FactHound have been researched by our staff.

Here's all you do:

Visit *www.facthound.com*

FactHound will fetch the best sites for you!

INDEX